Animal Bodie

WHOSE FEET ARE THOSE?

By Mary Griffin

Gareth Stevens
PUBLISHING

Please visit our website, www.garethstevens.com. For a free color catalog of all our high-quality books, call toll free 1-800-542-2595 or fax 1-877-542-2596.

Library of Congress Cataloging-in-Publication Data

Names: Griffin, Mary, 1978- author.
Title: Whose feet are those? / Mary Griffin.
Description: New York : Gareth Stevens Publishing, [2024] | Series: Animal bodies | Includes index.
Identifiers: LCCN 2022046886 (print) | LCCN 2022046887 (ebook) | ISBN 9781538286418 (library binding) | ISBN 9781538286401 (paperback) | ISBN 9781538286425 (ebook)
Subjects: LCSH: Foot–Juvenile literature.
Classification: LCC QL950.7 .G78 2024 (print) | LCC QL950.7 (ebook) | DDC 591.4–dc23/eng/20221018
LC record available at https://lccn.loc.gov/2022046886
LC ebook record available at https://lccn.loc.gov/2022046887

Published in 2024 by
Gareth Stevens Publishing
2544 Clinton Street
Buffalo, NY 14224

Designer: Tanya Dellaccio Keeney
Editor: Therese Shea

Photo credits: Cover, p.1 Andi111/Shutterstock.com; pp. 5, 7 EvgeniaSevryukova/Shutterstock.com; pp. 9, 11 Vlad G/Shutterstock.com; pp. 13, 15 Jane Rix/Shutterstock.com; pp. 17, 19 Linn Currie/Shutterstock.com; pp. 21, 23 Dave Denby Photography/Shutterstock.com.

Printed in the United States of America

CPSIA compliance information: Batch #CSGS24: For further information contact Gareth Stevens, at 1-800-542-2595.

Find us on

Contents

Let's look at animal feet!
Look at these webbed feet.

It's a duck!
It uses its feet to paddle.

Look at these clawed feet.

It's a bear!
Grizzly bears dig dens
with their claws.

Look at these big feet.

It's a rhino!
It has three toes
on each foot.

15

Look at this furry foot.

It's a cat!
Each foot has five or
six pads on it.

Look at this sticky foot.

It's a gecko.
Its feet help it climb walls!

Words to Know

claws

gecko

webbed

Index